WORKBOOK

For

Healing the Fragmented Selves of Trauma Survivors

Overcoming Internal Self-Alienation (A Practical Guide to Janina Fisher's Book)

Silver Quil Press

Copyright © 2023 by Silver Quil Press

This workbook is designed to complement and enhance the original book, While every effort has been made to ensure accuracy and effectiveness, this workbook is not intended to replace the original book, and its use is recommended in conjunction with reading the original text.

Table Of Contents

HOW TO USE THIS WORKBOOK

Welcome to the companion workbook for the book "Healing the Fragmented Selves of Trauma Survivors". This guide will walk you through how to effectively use this workbook to enhance your understanding, retention, and application of the key concepts presented in the main book.

- **Summary of the Main Book:** The first section of this workbook offers a concise summary of the main book. It encapsulates the core ideas and concepts presented, providing you with a quick reference guide.

- **Key Takeaways:** In each chapter, you'll find the most important points from the corresponding chapter of the main book. Take some time to reflect on these takeaways, considering how they relate to your own experiences and aspirations.

- **Self-Reflection Questions:** Following the Key Takeaways, you'll find a series of thought-provoking questions. Use these prompts to delve deeper into your understanding of the material and to connect it with your journey.

• **Positive Action Steps:** For each chapter, you'll discover actionable steps designed to help you apply the insights from the main book to your daily life. These plans are tailored to empower you to make positive changes and implement the knowledge gained.

• **Final Self-Assessment Questions:** As you near the end of this workbook, you'll find a set of questions aimed at gauging your progress and understanding. Be honest and thoughtful in your responses to get the most out of this self-assessment.

• **Journaling:** Use the provided space for journaling throughout the workbook. Documenting your thoughts and feelings can be a powerful way to track your progress. Take time to reflect on your responses. What insights have you gained? What changes do you aspire to make?

Read the main book to grab the core concepts and teachings, engage with the workbook by completing the exercises, answering the thought-provoking questions, and participating in the practical activities provided. Set aside some time each day to work on the workbook. Even if it's just for 15 minutes, regular practice will help you make the most of the experience. Find a quiet place where you won't be interrupted. This will help you focus on the material and your reflections.

You can work through the workbook at your own pace and in any order that you like. After each section, take a moment to review your responses and insights. Consider how you can integrate these learnings into your daily life moving forward. Remember, this workbook is a tool for ongoing personal development. Revisit it whenever you feel the need for inspiration, motivation, or a reminder of the valuable lessons learned from the main book.

Workbook Journal

_____

_____

_____

_____

_____

_____

_____

_____

_____

_____

_____

_____

SUMMARY OF THE MAIN BOOK

"Healing the Fragmented Selves of Trauma Survivors: Overcoming Internal Self-Alienation" by Janina Fisher is a comprehensive exploration of the impact of trauma on an individual's sense of self and the therapeutic approaches to healing the resulting internal fragmentation. The book delves into the complex nature of trauma and its profound effects on the psyche.

Fisher introduces the concept of internal self-alienation, where trauma survivors may experience a sense of disconnection and fragmentation within themselves. This fragmentation can manifest as a divided or conflicted sense of identity, making it challenging for individuals to integrate their experiences into a cohesive self-narrative.

Drawing on her expertise as a psychotherapist and incorporating insights from neuroscience, attachment theory, and somatic psychology, Fisher provides a nuanced understanding of the challenges faced by trauma survivors. She emphasizes the importance of recognizing and addressing the various parts of the self that may have become disconnected due to trauma.

The book outlines practical and effective therapeutic strategies to help individuals navigate the process of healing and integration. Fisher discusses the significance of establishing safety and trust in therapeutic relationships, creating a foundation for individuals to explore and make sense of their traumatic experiences.

Throughout the book, Fisher highlights the role of somatic experiencing and mindfulness techniques in addressing the physiological and embodied aspects of trauma. She explores how engaging with the body can be a powerful tool for promoting self-regulation and reconnecting with fragmented parts of the self.

Additionally, Fisher addresses the impact of trauma on memory, emphasizing the importance of understanding how memories are stored and retrieved in the context of trauma. She explores how certain therapeutic approaches, such as EMDR (Eye Movement

Desensitization and Reprocessing) and Internal Family Systems therapy, can be valuable in addressing memory-related challenges.

In summary, "Healing the Fragmented Selves of Trauma Survivors" provides a comprehensive guide for therapists and individuals alike to understand and address the complexities of trauma-induced self-alienation. Fisher's integrative approach, drawing from various therapeutic modalities, offers a roadmap for healing, integration, and the restoration of a more cohesive and resilient sense of self for trauma survivors.

Workbook Journal

_____

_____

_____

_____

_____

_____

_____

_____

_____

_____

_____

_____

_____

1. The Neurobiological Legacy of Trauma: How We Become Fragmented

Key Takeaways

1. Trauma can have profound effects on the brain, influencing its structure and function, and contributing to the fragmentation of the self.

2. The neurobiological response to trauma often involves dissociation and the development of survival strategies that can lead to a sense of internal self-alienation.

3. Trauma survivors may experience disruptions in memory, including fragmented and vivid recollections, impacting their ability to create a coherent life narrative.

4. Understanding the neurobiological aspects of trauma highlights the need for holistic therapeutic approaches that address both the psychological and physiological dimensions of healing.

Self-Reflection Questions

1. How do you recognize the signs of dissociation in your own experiences, and what impact do these moments have on your daily life?

_____

_____

_____

_____

_____

_____

_____

_____

_____

2. Consider the role of memory in your healing journey. How do fragmented memories influence your sense of self and the way you navigate relationships?

3. Reflect on the survival strategies you developed in response to trauma. In what ways have these strategies served you, and how might they contribute to a sense of internal self-alienation today?

_____

_____

_____

_____

_____

_____

_____

_____

Positive Action Steps

1. Begin integrating mindful awareness into your daily routine. Notice moments of dissociation without judgment, bringing gentle attention to your thoughts and sensations.

2. Dedicate time to journaling about your memories, paying attention to any patterns or emotions that arise. Consider seeking professional guidance to navigate challenging memories.

3. Explore holistic approaches to healing, such as somatic therapy or mindfulness practices. Identify one specific holistic modality that resonates with you and take a step toward incorporating it into your self-care routine.

Workbook Journal

_____

_____

_____

_____

_____

_____

_____

_____

_____

_____

_____

_____

2. Understanding Parts, Understanding Traumatic Responses

Key Takeaways

1. Acknowledging the multiplicity of self is crucial in understanding how trauma can lead to the emergence of distinct and often conflicting parts within an individual.

2. Traumatic responses can give rise to internal conflicts between protective parts and parts that hold the emotional pain of the trauma, contributing to a sense of internal self-alienation.

3. Parts emerge as adaptive survival strategies in response to trauma, helping individuals cope with overwhelming experiences and navigate their environment.

4. Developing compassion for the different parts of yourself is a foundational step in healing, fostering integration rather than internal conflict.

Self-Reflection Questions

1. How do you notice the presence of different parts within yourself, especially during moments of stress or emotional intensity?

_____

_____

_____

_____

_____

_____

_____

_____

2. Consider the protective parts that have emerged in response to trauma. How do these parts manifest in your thoughts, behaviors, and relationships?

_____

_____

_____

_____

_____

_____

_____

_____

_____

3. Reflect on a recent internal conflict you experienced. How did different parts of yourself contribute to the conflict, and what needs did each part try to meet?

Positive Action Steps

1. Engage in a part recognition exercise by journaling about the various aspects of yourself. Identify at least three distinct parts and acknowledge the role each plays in your life.

2. Practice compassionate internal dialogue. When you notice conflicting parts within yourself, approach them with curiosity and kindness, acknowledging their efforts to protect and cope.

3. Explore externalizing parts through artistic expression. Use drawing, painting, or another creative outlet to visually represent different aspects of yourself. This can provide a tangible and symbolic way to engage with your internal world.

Workbook Journal

_____

_____

_____

_____

_____

_____

_____

_____

_____

_____

_____

_____

3. Changing Roles for Client and Therapist

Key Takeaways

1. The therapeutic relationship is a collaborative partnership where the client actively engages in exploring and understanding the fragmented parts of themselves alongside the therapist.

2. The traditional power dynamics in therapy shift towards a more egalitarian approach, empowering the client to take an active role in their healing journey.

3. Recognizing the client as the expert on their own experience allows for a more client-centered and empowering therapeutic process.

4. Establishing a safe therapeutic space is foundational for the client to explore vulnerable and fragmented aspects of themselves.

Self-Reflection Questions

1. How do you experience the collaborative nature of therapy, and in what ways does this dynamic contribute to your sense of agency in the healing process?

_____

_____

_____

_____

_____

_____

_____

_____

2. Consider the shifting power dynamics in therapy. How does this shift impact your ability to engage with and trust the therapeutic process?

_____

_____

_____

_____

_____

_____

_____

_____

_____

3. Reflect on the concept of safety in therapy. How do you experience safety in the therapeutic relationship, and how does this contribute to your willingness to explore vulnerable aspects of yourself?

Positive Action Steps

1. Take a moment to communicate with your therapist about your preferences for collaboration in the therapeutic process. Discuss any adjustments or specific approaches that may enhance your engagement.

2. Use journaling as a tool to reflect on your evolving role in therapy. Note any insights or shifts in your perception of yourself and the therapeutic process.

3. Collaborate with your therapist to set and revisit therapeutic goals. Clarify your aspirations for healing and integration, and work together to establish tangible steps towards those goals.

Workbook Journal

---

4. Learning to See Our "Selves": An Introduction to Working with Parts

Key Takeaways

1. The chapter emphasizes the importance of exploring the internal landscape, recognizing and understanding the different parts that make up your sense of self.

2. Learning to identify and differentiate between protective parts and parts holding traumatic memories is essential for the process of integration.

3. Approaching your internal parts with curiosity and non-judgment creates a foundation for self-compassion and understanding.

4. Recognizing that the journey of integrating fragmented selves is an ongoing, lifelong process, allowing for patience and self-acceptance.

Self-Reflection Questions

1. How do you currently perceive your internal landscape, and what might be preventing you from fully exploring and understanding the various parts that make up your sense of self?

_____

_____

_____

_____

_____

_____

_____

_____

2. Consider the process of identifying different internal parts. How do you approach this task, and what emotions arise as you begin to recognize the complexity of your internal world?

_____

_____

_____

_____

_____

_____

_____

_____

3. Reflect on the concept of integration as a lifelong process. How does this perspective influence your expectations for your healing journey, and how might it impact your commitment to self-discovery and growth?

Positive Action Steps

1. Engage in an exercise to map out your internal landscape. Use drawings, diagrams, or descriptive words to represent different aspects of yourself.

2. Dedicate a journaling session to exploring one specific internal part in-depth. Approach this exploration with a sense of curiosity, noting its role and significance in your life.

3. Incorporate mindfulness practices into your daily routine to foster a sense of presence and acceptance. Mindfully observe your thoughts and emotions without judgment, creating space for the integration process to unfold.

Workbook Journal

_____

_____

_____

_____

_____

_____

_____

_____

_____

_____

_____

5. Befriending Our Parts: Sowing the Seeds of Compassion

Key Takeaways

1. The chapter underscores the importance of cultivating compassion towards the different parts of yourself, fostering a non-judgmental and understanding relationship.

2. Befriending your parts involves acknowledging and appreciating the protective functions they serve, even if these functions initially arose as survival strategies.

3. Compassion creates an environment in which internal parts can work together more cohesively, contributing to a sense of wholeness.

4. The chapter emphasizes the need to challenge and transform inner criticism, replacing it with a compassionate and validating internal dialogue.

Self-Reflection Questions

1. How do you currently approach the idea of befriending different parts of yourself, and what challenges or resistances might you encounter in this process?

_____

_____

_____

_____

_____

_____

_____

_____

2. Consider the protective functions of your internal parts. How might recognizing and appreciating these functions contribute to a more compassionate relationship with yourself?

_____

_____

_____

_____

_____

_____

_____

_____

_____

3. Reflect on the presence of inner criticism in your internal dialogue. How does this criticism impact your overall well-being, and what steps can you take to challenge and transform it into a more compassionate and supportive voice?

_____

_____

_____

_____

_____

_____

_____

_____

Positive Action Steps

1. Engage in an exercise of writing compassionate letters to specific parts of yourself. Acknowledge their efforts, express gratitude, and explore ways to work together more harmoniously.

2. Practice mindfulness to become more aware of your inner critic. When the inner critic arises, consciously redirect your thoughts toward self-compassionate and affirming statements.

3. Develop a daily routine of self-validation. Identify and celebrate your achievements, no matter how small, and intentionally acknowledge the positive qualities within yourself.

Workbook Journal

6. Complications of Treatment: Traumatic Attachment

Key Takeaways

1. The chapter explores how past traumatic attachments can influence the therapeutic relationship, affecting trust, connection, and the ability to engage in the healing process.

2. Traumatic attachment patterns from the past may be repeated in the therapeutic relationship, requiring awareness and therapeutic exploration for resolution.

3. Understanding and navigating transference (client's feelings toward the therapist) and countertransference (therapist's feelings toward the client) are essential for overcoming complications in treatment.

4. Despite challenges, the therapeutic alliance can be repaired through open communication, validation, and collaborative exploration of attachment dynamics.

Self-Reflection Questions

1. How do you notice the influence of past traumatic attachments in your current therapeutic relationship, and in what ways might it impact your ability to trust and connect with your therapist?

_____

_____

_____

_____

_____

_____

_____

_____

_____

2. Consider the concept of repetition of attachment patterns. How do you observe these patterns playing out in your therapeutic interactions, and what emotions or challenges arise as a result?

_____

_____

_____

_____

_____

_____

_____

_____

_____

3. Reflect on the dynamics of transference and countertransference in your therapeutic relationship. How might these dynamics be influencing your perception of the therapist and the therapeutic process?

_____

_____

_____

_____

_____

_____

_____

_____

Positive Action Steps

1. Initiate open and honest communication with your therapist about any challenges or concerns related to trust, attachment, or the therapeutic relationship. Discussing these issues can contribute to a deeper understanding and resolution.

2. Dedicate a journaling session to exploring your attachment patterns, both in the past and present. Identify any recurring themes or emotions and consider how these patterns may be influencing your therapeutic experience.

3. Work collaboratively with your therapist to explore and understand attachment dynamics. Engage in exercises or discussions aimed at resolving past attachment wounds and fostering a more secure and trusting therapeutic alliance.

Workbook Journal

7. Working with Suicidal, Self-Destructive, Eating Disordered, and Addicted Parts

Key Takeaways

1. The chapter highlights the importance of understanding self-destructive behaviors, such as suicidality, eating disorders, and addiction, as coping mechanisms developed in response to trauma.

2. Working with these parts requires a compassionate exploration of the underlying pain and unmet needs that drive self-destructive behaviors.

3. The goal is to integrate and collaborate with these parts, fostering healthier coping strategies and addressing the root causes of the destructive behaviors.

4. Establishing safety plans and crisis interventions is crucial when working with parts that engage in self-destructive behaviors.

Self-Reflection Questions

1. How do you observe the presence of self-destructive behaviors within yourself, and what emotions or triggers might be associated with these behaviors?

_____

_____

_____

_____

_____

_____

_____

_____

2. Consider the underlying pain and unmet needs that drive self-destructive parts. How might addressing these needs contribute to a more compassionate and effective approach to healing?

_____

_____

_____

_____

_____

_____

_____

_____

_____

3. Reflect on your current safety planning and crisis interventions. How do these strategies support you in moments of distress, and what additional resources or practices might enhance your safety plan?

_____

_____

_____

_____

_____

_____

_____

_____

Positive Action Steps

1. Work collaboratively with your therapist to update and enhance your safety plan. Consider incorporating new strategies or resources that align with your evolving understanding of your self-destructive parts.

2. Explore artistic expression as a tool to communicate and understand the experiences of self-destructive parts. Use drawing, painting, or writing to externalize and process the emotions associated with these parts.

3. Integrate mindful coping strategies into your daily routine. Identify activities or practices that promote a sense of safety and grounding, providing alternatives to self-destructive behaviors during challenging moments.

Workbook Journal

_____

_____

_____

_____

_____

_____

_____

_____

_____

_____

_____

_____

8. Treatment Challenges: Dissociative Systems and Disorders

Key Takeaways

1. The chapter emphasizes the complexity of dissociative systems and disorders, where individuals may experience fragmentation of identity, memory loss, and altered states of consciousness.

2. Treatment involves a careful and gradual process of integrating dissociative parts to facilitate a more cohesive and unified sense of self.

3. Establishing safety and stabilization is a crucial first step in working with dissociative systems, providing a secure foundation for exploration and healing.

4. Successful treatment often requires collaboration between the client and therapist, as well as a multidisciplinary approach that may involve psychiatrists, neurologists, and other specialists.

Self-Reflection Questions

1. How do you notice the presence of dissociative experiences within yourself, and what challenges or disruptions might these experiences bring to your daily life?

_____

_____

_____

_____

_____

_____

_____

_____

2. Consider the idea of integrating dissociative parts. How might this process contribute to a more cohesive and unified sense of self, and what fears or resistances might arise as you contemplate this integration?

_____

_____

_____

_____

_____

_____

_____

_____

_____

3. Reflect on the concept of safety and stabilization in your therapeutic journey. How do these factors contribute to your ability to explore and address dissociative experiences, and what additional supports might enhance your sense of safety?

_____

_____

_____

_____

_____

_____

_____

_____

Positive Action Steps

1. Engage in open communication with your therapist about any challenges or concerns related to dissociative experiences. Collaboratively explore strategies to enhance safety and stabilization during therapy sessions.

2. Incorporate mindful grounding techniques into your daily routine. Identify practices that help you stay present and connected during moments of dissociation, fostering a sense of stability.

3. Take an active role in your treatment by educating yourself about dissociative systems and disorders. Advocate for your needs and collaborate with your therapist to develop a comprehensive treatment plan that addresses the complexity of your experiences.

Workbook Journal

_____

_____

_____

_____

_____

_____

_____

_____

_____

_____

_____

9. Repairing the Past: Embracing Our Selves

Key Takeaways

1. The chapter emphasizes the significance of cultivating self-compassion as a vital aspect of the healing journey, fostering acceptance and understanding of all parts of the self.

2. Repairing the past involves a process of reparenting, nurturing wounded parts of yourself with kindness and care that may have been lacking in earlier experiences.

3. The goal is to move towards integration and wholeness, embracing all aspects of the self, including those that may have been rejected or disowned due to trauma.

4. Embracing your selves involves a transformative process where self-acceptance and self-love contribute to healing past wounds and fostering a more positive relationship with yourself.

Self-Reflection Questions

1. How do you currently approach the practice of self-compassion, and in what ways might cultivating a more compassionate relationship with all parts of yourself contribute to your overall well-being?

_____

_____

_____

_____

_____

_____

_____

_____

2. Consider the concept of reparenting. How might nurturing wounded parts with kindness and care influence your internal dialogue, and what challenges or resistances might arise in this process?

_____

_____

_____

_____

_____

_____

_____

_____

_____

3. Reflect on the idea of integration and wholeness. How does the prospect of embracing all aspects of yourself

contribute to a sense of internal unity, and what steps can you take to foster this integration?

_____

_____

_____

_____

_____

_____

_____

_____

Positive Action Steps

1. Establish a daily self-compassion practice. Engage in activities that nurture and validate different parts of yourself, fostering a compassionate and accepting internal environment.

2. Create reparenting rituals. Identify specific actions or affirmations that symbolize the nurturing care you may have missed in the past, and incorporate these into your daily or weekly routine.

3. Dedicate time to integration journaling. Reflect on moments when you felt fragmented or disconnected and explore ways to integrate those experiences into a broader understanding of yourself.

Workbook Journal

_____

_____

_____

_____

_____

_____

_____

_____

_____

_____

_____

10. Restoring What Was Lost: Deepening the Connection To Our Young Selves

Key Takeaways

1. The chapter emphasizes the importance of deepening your connection with your younger selves, understanding their needs, and providing the care and support they may have lacked.

2. Restoring what was lost involves actively engaging in the healing of the wounded inner child, acknowledging past traumas, and fostering a sense of safety and nurturance.

3. Integrating childlike qualities, such as playfulness and curiosity, into your present self contributes to a more balanced and resilient sense of identity.

4. Nurturing the innocence within allows for the rediscovery of joy, wonder, and spontaneity, fostering a deeper connection with your authentic self.

Self-Reflection Questions

1. How do you currently perceive and connect with your younger selves, and in what ways might deepening this connection contribute to your overall sense of well-being?

_____

_____

_____

_____

_____

_____

_____

_____

2. Consider the concept of healing the wounded child. How might acknowledging and addressing past traumas foster a sense of safety and nurturance in your current experiences, and what emotions or challenges might arise during this process?

_____

_____

_____

_____

_____

_____

_____

_____

_____

3. Reflect on the integration of childlike qualities. How does embracing playfulness and curiosity contribute to your present identity, and how might these qualities enhance your resilience and overall life satisfaction?

_____

_____

_____

_____

_____

_____

_____

_____

Positive Action Steps

1. Initiate an inner child journaling practice. Write letters to your younger selves, expressing care, understanding, and support. Use this practice to nurture and deepen your connection with the different stages of your development.

2. Engage in creative expression as a means of connecting with your inner child. Incorporate activities such as drawing, painting, or storytelling to give voice to the emotions and experiences of your younger selves.

3. Integrate mindful play into your routine. Dedicate time to activities that bring joy and tap into a sense of wonder. This could include activities you enjoyed in childhood or new experiences that evoke a childlike sense of exploration and delight.

Workbook Journal

_____

_____

_____

_____

_____

_____

_____

_____

_____

_____

_____

_____

11. Safety and Welcome: The Experience of EarnedSecure Attachment

Key Takeaways

1. The chapter explores the concept of earned secure attachment, emphasizing the transformative potential for individuals to develop a sense of safety and security through therapeutic relationships.

2. Earned secure attachment involves a gradual rebuilding of trust in relationships, providing a corrective emotional experience that contrasts with past traumatic attachments.

3. The experience of earned secure attachment allows individuals to internalize a sense of safety and welcome, fostering a more stable and positive sense of self.

4. The therapeutic relationship serves as a crucial healing force, offering opportunities for connection, understanding, and the development of a secure base.

Self-Reflection Questions

1. How do you currently experience safety and welcome in your relationships, and in what ways might the concept of earned secure attachment contribute to a deeper sense of security in your connections?

_____

_____

_____

_____

_____

_____

_____

_____

2. Consider the process of rebuilding trust. How might this process impact your ability to engage in meaningful and fulfilling relationships, and what steps can you take to nurture the gradual development of trust?

_____

_____

_____

_____

_____

_____

_____

_____

_____

_____

3. Reflect on the therapeutic relationship as a healing force. How has your experience in therapy contributed to your sense of connection and security, and how might you further cultivate the therapeutic relationship as a source of healing?

_____

_____

_____

_____

_____

_____

_____

_____

Positive Action Steps

1. Initiate open communication with your therapist about your experiences of safety and trust in the therapeutic relationship. Share insights into how the therapeutic connection contributes to your sense of security.

2. Collaborate with your therapist to explore attachment patterns that may be influencing your current relationships. Identify specific actions or strategies that can support the gradual rebuilding of trust.

3. Engage in mindful reflection on safety in your relationships. Regularly take moments to acknowledge and internalize feelings of safety and welcome, fostering a deeper sense of security within yourself.

Workbook Journal

_____

_____

_____

_____

_____

_____

_____

_____

_____

_____

_____

_____

Appendix A: Five Steps to "Unblending"

Key Takeaways

1. The five steps provide a structured approach for intentionally separating and understanding different parts of yourself, fostering greater self-awareness.

2. "Unblending" is a tool for exploring internal dynamics and creating a pathway towards integration, allowing fragmented selves to be acknowledged and understood.

3. The process involves mindful engagement with various aspects of your internal experience, promoting a more conscious and compassionate relationship with different parts.

4. By following these steps, individuals can work towards internal harmony, where different aspects of the self coexist and collaborate more cohesively.

Self-Reflection Questions

1. How can you apply the five steps to "Unblending" in your current experiences to promote a deeper understanding and connection with different parts of yourself?

_____

_____

_____

_____

_____

_____

_____

_____

2. Consider the intentional exploration involved. How might this process contribute to a more conscious and aware relationship with your internal dynamics, and what insights can you gain from engaging in this intentional exploration?

_____

_____

_____

_____

_____

_____

_____

_____

_____

3. Reflect on the idea of promoting internal harmony. How does the concept of "Unblending" align with your desire for a more cohesive and integrated sense of self?

_____

_____

_____

_____

_____

_____

_____

_____

Positive Action Steps

1. Choose a specific situation or emotion to experiment with the "Unblending" process. Apply the five steps mindfully and observe the impact on your self-awareness and internal dynamics.

2. Dedicate a journaling session to reflect on your experiences with "Unblending." Reflect on any insights, obstacles, or changes in your perspective as you embark on this deliberate separation

3. If you are in therapy, consider sharing your exploration of "Unblending" with your therapist. Discuss how this process aligns with your therapeutic goals and explore ways to integrate it into your ongoing work.

Workbook Journal

_____

_____

_____

_____

_____

_____

_____

_____

_____

_____

_____

_____

Appendix B: Meditation Circle for Parts

Key Takeaways

1. The Meditation Circle for Parts is a guided meditation technique designed to facilitate connection and communication with different internal parts.

2. This meditation provides a safe and exploratory space for individuals to engage with their fragmented selves in a mindful and supportive manner.

3. The guided meditation aims to promote a deeper inner connection, allowing individuals to cultivate a sense of presence and awareness within their internal landscape.

4. By participating in the Meditation Circle for Parts, individuals can engage in a mindful exploration of their internal world, fostering a more conscious and compassionate relationship with their inner selves.

Self-Reflection Questions

1. How does the Meditation Circle for Parts contribute to your experience of a safe and exploratory space within yourself?

_____

_____

_____

_____

_____

_____

_____

_____

2. Consider the concept of inner connection. How might this guided meditation promote a deeper sense of presence and awareness within your internal landscape?

_____

_____

_____

_____

_____

_____

_____

_____

_____

3. Reflect on the idea of mindful engagement. How can the Meditation Circle for Parts support your ongoing efforts to cultivate a conscious and compassionate relationship with your inner selves?

_____

_____

_____

_____

_____

_____

_____

_____

Positive Action Steps

1. Integrate the Meditation Circle for Parts into your regular mindfulness or meditation practice. Dedicate specific sessions to this guided meditation to deepen your connection with internal parts.

2. After each meditation session, take time to reflect on your inner experiences. Journal about any insights, emotions, or shifts in perception that arise during or after the practice.

3. If comfortable, share your experiences with the Meditation Circle for Parts with a therapist or support system. Discuss how this practice contributes to your overall sense of self-awareness and well-being.

Workbook Journal

_____

_____

_____

_____

_____

_____

_____

_____

_____

_____

_____

_____

_____

Appendix C: Internal Dialogue Technique

Key Takeaways

1. The Internal Dialogue Technique provides a practical tool for facilitating communication between different parts of the self.

2. Engaging in internal dialogue promotes understanding among different parts, fostering a more cohesive internal environment.

3. This technique encourages collaboration between fragmented selves, contributing to the integration of various aspects of one's identity.

4. Through internal dialogue, individuals empower themselves to explore and address their inner dynamics, promoting self-reflection and insight.

Self-Reflection Questions

1. How can the Internal Dialogue Technique be applied to facilitate communication and understanding among different parts of yourself?

_____

_____

_____

_____

_____

_____

_____

_____

2. Consider the concept of collaborative integration. In what ways might engaging in internal dialogue contribute to a more cohesive and integrated sense of self?

_____

_____

_____

_____

_____

_____

_____

_____

_____

3. Reflect on the idea of empowering self-reflection. How does the Internal Dialogue Technique provide a tool for exploring and addressing your inner dynamics in a self-reflective manner?

_____

_____

_____

_____

_____

_____

_____

_____

Positive Action Steps

1. Set aside specific times for regular internal dialogue sessions. Use this technique to facilitate communication and understanding among different parts of yourself.

2. Keep a journal to record internal conversations that arise during the Internal Dialogue Technique. Document insights, emotions, and any shifts in perspective that occur.

3. If you are in therapy, discuss the themes and insights from your internal dialogues with your therapist. Explore how this technique aligns with your therapeutic goals and contributes to your overall healing journey.

Workbook Journal

_____

_____

_____

_____

_____

_____

_____

_____

_____

_____

_____

_____

Appendix D: Treatment Paradigm for Internal Attachment Repair

Key Takeaways

1. The treatment paradigm offers a structured framework for internal attachment repair, addressing the impact of trauma on attachment patterns.

2. It advocates for a multidimensional approach, recognizing the complexity of internal attachment dynamics and incorporating various therapeutic strategies.

3. The paradigm focuses on healing and strengthening internal relationships, fostering a more secure and supportive internal environment.

4. Successful implementation of the treatment paradigm involves collaboration between the individual and therapist, emphasizing the importance of the therapeutic relationship.

Self-Reflection Questions

1. How does the treatment paradigm resonate with your understanding of internal attachment repair, and in what ways might it provide a comprehensive approach to healing?

_____

_____

_____

_____

_____

_____

_____

_____

_____

2. Consider the multidimensional approach. How can you actively engage in various therapeutic strategies to address the complexity of your internal attachment dynamics?

_____

_____

_____

_____

_____

_____

_____

_____

_____

3. Reflect on the collaborative therapeutic effort. How does the treatment paradigm emphasize the importance of collaboration between you and your therapist, and what steps can you take to enhance your collaboration in the therapeutic process?

_____

_____

_____

_____

_____

_____

_____

_____

Positive Action Steps

1. Work with your therapist to collaboratively set goals based on the treatment paradigm. Discuss specific strategies and interventions that align with the multidimensional approach outlined in the paradigm.

2. Establish a routine for evaluating your progress within the treatment paradigm. Regularly assess the impact of different therapeutic strategies on your internal attachment dynamics and make adjustments as needed.

3. Foster open communication with your therapist regarding your experiences with the treatment paradigm. Share insights, challenges, and any shifts in your internal relationships, creating a space for ongoing collaboration and adjustment.

Workbook Journal

Appendix E: Dissociative Experiences Log

Key Takeaways

1. The Dissociative Experiences Log is a practical tool for tracking and understanding dissociative experiences.

2. By using the log, individuals can gain insights into the frequency, triggers, and emotional states associated with dissociation, facilitating a more comprehensive understanding of these experiences.

3. The log serves as a valuable resource for therapy, providing therapists with concrete information to tailor interventions and explore dissociative patterns more effectively.

4. Regular use of the log promotes self-awareness and a deeper understanding of the factors contributing to dissociative experiences.

Self-Reflection Questions

1. How can the Dissociative Experiences Log be integrated into your routine to track and understand your dissociative experiences more effectively?

_____

_____

_____

_____

_____

_____

_____

_____

2. Consider the insights gained. How might tracking the frequency, triggers, and emotional states associated with dissociation contribute to a deeper understanding of your experiences?

---

3. Reflect on the idea of promoting self-awareness. In what ways does the Dissociative Experiences Log serve as a tool for promoting self-awareness, and how can this awareness enhance your overall well-being?

_____

_____

_____

_____

_____

_____

_____

_____

Positive Action Steps

1. Set up a regular routine for using the Dissociative Experiences Log. Dedicate specific times to record your experiences and be consistent in tracking the relevant information.

2. Periodically review your log entries and reflect on the patterns and insights that emerge. Consider sharing these reflections with your therapist to enrich your therapeutic discussions.

3. Work collaboratively with your therapist to develop interventions based on the information from the Dissociative Experiences Log. Explore strategies to address triggers and enhance your coping mechanisms in response to dissociative experiences.

Workbook Journal

_____

_____

_____

_____

_____

_____

_____

_____

_____

_____

_____

_____

Appendix F: The Four Befriending Questions

Key Takeaways

1. The Four Befriending Questions provide a framework for compassionate inquiry, encouraging individuals to explore the needs, fears, and motivations of different parts.

2. By engaging with these questions, individuals promote self-understanding and develop a more empathetic and supportive relationship with their internal selves.

3. The befriending questions contribute to the overall process of integration by acknowledging and befriending different aspects of the self.

4. The questions facilitate the development of a supportive and nurturing internal dialogue, fostering a sense of connection and acceptance.

Self-Reflection Questions

1. How can the Four Befriending Questions be incorporated into your self-reflection practices to promote compassionate inquiry into the needs and motivations of different parts of yourself?

---

2. Consider the concept of self-understanding. In what ways might engaging with these questions enhance your understanding of the various aspects of your internal world?

_____

_____

_____

_____

_____

_____

_____

_____

3. Reflect on the idea of a supportive internal dialogue. How do the Four Befriending Questions contribute to creating a more supportive and nurturing internal dialogue, and how can this influence your overall well-being?

_____

_____

_____

_____

_____

_____

_____

_____

_____

Positive Action Steps

1. Integrate the Four Befriending Questions into your regular self-inquiry practices. Dedicate time to reflect on these questions, exploring the needs and motivations of different parts.

2. Use journaling as a tool to respond to the Four Befriending Questions. Document your reflections and insights, creating a tangible record of your evolving understanding and relationship with your internal selves.

3. Discuss your experiences with the Four Befriending Questions with your therapist. Explore how these questions align with your therapeutic goals and consider ways to integrate them into your ongoing therapeutic work.

Workbook Journal

_____

_____

_____

_____

_____

_____

_____

_____

_____

_____

_____

FINAL SELF-ASSESSMENT QUESTIONS

1. Did you consistently meet the set goals and objectives throughout the workbook?

2. Were you able to apply the concepts and techniques learned in the workbook to real-life situations or tasks?

_____

_____

_____

_____

_____

_____

_____

_____

3. Did you seek clarification or additional resources when you encountered challenges or difficulties?

4. Identify one new skill or technique you've learned from this workbook. How have you practiced or applied it in your life?

_____

_____

_____

_____

_____

_____

_____

_____

5. Envision your future self based on the insights gained from this workbook. What specific actions or habits will you continue to cultivate for ongoing personal development?

_____

_____

_____

_____

_____

_____

_____

_____

_____

6. Imagine yourself a year from now, having fully embraced the teachings of this workbook. What changes do you envision in your life, and how will you continue to cultivate personal growth and development?

_____

_____

_____

_____

_____

_____

_____

_____

7. Did you collaborate or seek feedback from peers or mentors to enhance your understanding and performance?

_____

_____

_____

_____

_____

_____

_____

_____

Workbook Journal

_____

_____

_____

_____

_____

_____

_____

_____

_____

_____

_____

Workbook Journal

Made in the USA
Coppell, TX
24 June 2025

51099101R00069